The Quota

The Welsh Quotation Book

A Literary Companion

Edited by
ROGER THOMAS

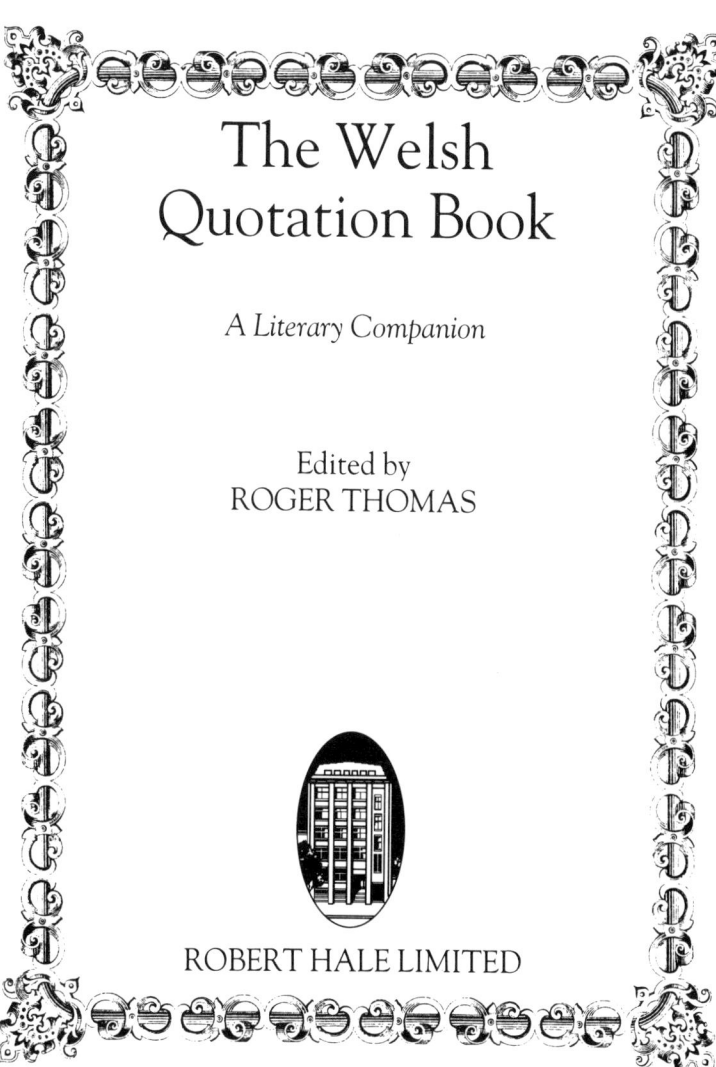

ROBERT HALE LIMITED

Preface and selection © Roger Thomas 1994
First published in Great Britain 1994

ISBN 0 7090 5168 9

Robert Hale Limited
Clerkenwell House
Clerkenwell Green
London EC1R 0HT

2 4 6 8 10 9 7 5 3 1

The right of Roger Thomas to be identified as
author of this work has been asserted by him
in accordance with the Copyright, Designs
and Patents Act 1988.

Photoset in Goudy by
Derek Doyle & Associates, Mold, Clwyd.
Printed and bound by WBC Ltd,
Bridgend, Mid-Glamorgan, Wales

Preface

Wales, with its manifold nuances, is as constant as a chameleon. I should know, for I have been an inhabitant for most of my life, yet still find it impossible to pin down its elusive character. There are, of course, the well-known – and well-worn – Welsh clichés: the music-hall Welshman, the flat cap, the heroic collier, the rugby, the harp and the leek. But those who really know Wales treat them with the contempt they deserve, for there are almost as many definitions of Wales as there are Welsh people.

Although, from the other side of Offa's Dyke, Wales might seem a neatly packaged, homogenous country populated by sheep and male-voice choirs, the view from within is confusing, contradictory and kaleidoscopic. There are Welsh-speaking farmers and English-speaking factory workers, English-speaking farmers and Welsh-speaking civil servants, chapel-goers and Catholics, nationalists and internationalists, frustrated devolutionists and ardent royalists, Eisteddfod lovers and those who regard traditional Welsh culture as high comedy. Sure, we are all Welsh. On that point, at least, we can all agree. Just don't ask us to form a consensus view on the definitive nature of Welshness.

This capacity to disagree amongst ourselves was a trait first spotted by the medieval traveller and chronicler, Giraldus

The Welsh Quotation Book

Cambrensis (Gerald of Wales). Giraldus, Wales's first travel writer, was later followed by luminaries such as Daniel Defoe, Samuel Johnson, William Wordsworth and J.M.W. Turner, all of whom gave us their opinions – sometimes praiseworthy, sometimes unflattering – of Wales.

But for the best insights into the contradictions and complexities of Wales and the Welsh character we have to look to indigenous writers. Dylan Thomas touched on the differences with the dichotomous 'ugly, lovely' description of his home town of Swansea. Some writers use unashamedly romantic prose to conjure up a mystical, Celtic Wales that may or may not exist. Others write in a gritty, down-to-earth manner about the toil and hardships of industrial life and marginal farming. Some extol the sense of sharing and community which they experience in Wales. Others criticize the narrowness – and nosiness that is often a corollary of such closeness.

In this collection, you will see Wales from all angles – from the perspective of the outsider, and from the dissenting views of those within who pedal their particular notion of Welshness. The funny thing is, despite the arguments, few of us would consider living anywhere else.

Acknowledgements

I am most grateful to the following authors, agents and publishers for permission to quote substantial extracts of prose and poetry.

David Higham Associates: extracts from *Reminiscences of Childhood, Under Milk Wood* and *The Poems* by Dylan Thomas, published by J.M. Dent; Gomer Press: extract from Idris Davies's *Collected Poems*; D. Brown and Sons Ltd, Bridgend, Mid Glamorgan: extracts from *High on Hope* by Gwyn Thomas; Michael Joseph Ltd: extract from *How Green Was My Valley* by Richard Llewellyn (Michael Joseph 1939); poetry and prose by Ernest Rhys, published by J.M. Dent; and Jan Morris.

I would also like to thank Richard Keen for his invaluable advice.

Every effort has been made to contact all relevant copyright holders. I offer my apologies wherever this has proved to be impossible.

Their Lord they will praise,
Their speech they will keep,
Their land they will lose,
Except wild Wales.
> Ancient legend predicting the fate of the Britons

The Britons for the most part have a natural hatred for the English ...
> BEDE
> 731

The Welsh are entirely different in nation, language, laws and habits, judgements and customs.
> THE BISHOP OF ST DAVID'S
> 12th-century letter to the Pope

The Welsh Quotation Book

Everyone's home is open to all, and there is no need for travellers even to ask for accommodation. You just walk straight into the house and hand over your weapons for safekeeping: then someone immediately offers you water, and if you wash your feet, that means that you want to stay for the night.
> GIRALDUS CAMBRENSIS (GERALD OF WALES)
> *Description of Wales*, 12th century

A WELSH CORACLE.

... are made of twigs, not oblong nor pointed, but almost round, or rather triangular, covered both within and without with raw hides. When a salmon thrown into one of these boats strikes it hard with its tail, he often oversets it, and endangers both the vessel and its navigator.
> GIRALDUS CAMBRENSIS (GERALD OF WALES)
> Description of the coracle, a tiny fishing-boat which is still used in certain parts of Wales

The Welsh Quotation Book

The Coracles, the native boats, similar to those employed by the ancient Britons, are used by fishermen on the Conway. These boats are made of wickerwork covered with skins or strong canvas. They are very light, and when their owners have completed their work, they strap them on their backs and march home with them.
JOHN TILLOTSON
Picturesque Scenery in Wales, 1860

If thou desirest to die, eat cabbage in August.

Good are a salmon and a sermon in Lent.

A light dinner and less supper, sound sleep, and a long life.

A cold mouth and warm feet will live long.

Supper can kill more than the Physicians of Myddfai can cure.

The Welsh Quotation Book

To extract a Tooth without Pain: Take some newts, by some called lizards, and those nasty beetles which are found in ferns during summer, calcine them in an iron pot, and make a powder thereof. Wet the forefinger of the right hand, insert it in the powder, and apply it to the tooth frequently, refraining from spitting it off, when the tooth will fall away without pain. It is proven.

To oblige a Man to confess what He has done wrong: Take a frog alive from the water. Extract its tongue and put him back again in the water. Lay this same tongue on the heart of the sleeping man, and he will confess his deeds in his sleep.
> Advice from the physicians of Myddfai
> Medieval

> Valeyes bringeth forth food,
> And hilles metal right good,
> Col groweth under lond,
> And grass above at the hond,
> There lyme is copious,
> And sclattes also for hous.
>> RANULF HIGDEN
>> *Polychronicon (De Wallia)*, 1387

> Many a time I've thought a harper
> would make the most untiring lover
> for his plucking of the strings
> would sweeten dawns and evenings.
>> ANONYMOUS
>> Stanza in praise of the harp

The Welsh Quotation Book

The Welsh Quotation Book

The Welsh habit of revolt against the English is a long-standing madness ...
> ANONYMOUS
> 14th-century observation

Nor can I easily be persuaded that nature hath given such splendour to the rocks in vain, and that this flower should be without fruit, if anyone would take the pains to penetrate deeply into the bowels of the earth; if anyone, I say, would extract honey from the rocks, and oil from the stone. Indeed many riches of nature lie concealed through inattention, which the diligence of posterity will bring to light.
> AN UNKNOWN CLASSICAL WRITER
> Observation quoted by medieval traveller Giraldus Cambrensis (Gerald of Wales)

Nor do I think that any other nation than that of Wales ... shall, on the day of severe examination before the supreme Judge, answer for this corner of the earth.
> AN UNKNOWN WELSHMAN TO HENRY II
> 12th century

I would not wish to live, my darling
if I may not obtain my lovely bashful girl.
This is the cause of my affliction:
sweet Morfudd, I shall die.
> DAFYDD AP GWILYM
> Medieval poet

The Welsh Quotation Book

What reward have I had from following her?
It were high time to have done with the girl.
    DAFYDD AP GWILYM
    Writing about Morfudd

The ancient history of Wales is a calendar of usurpations, depredations, and murders.
    HENRY PENRUDDOCKE WYNDHAM
    A Gentleman's Tour through Monmouthshire and Wales, 1797

… good, and victuals nothing deare,
Each place is filde with plentie all the yeare,
The ground manurde, the graine doth so increase
That thousands live in wealth and blessed peace …
Wales in this day (behold throughout the sheares)
In better state than was these hundred yeeres …
    THOMAS CHURCHYARD
    1587

Some Welsh folk are so foolish
Striving to ape the English;
Young and old are trying to be
Like gentry – what mock polish!
    THOMAS EDWARDS
    18th century

The Welsh Quotation Book

When my life was thrifty, thrifty,
Soon my one sheep grew to fifty;
After that I lived for fun
And now my flock is back to one.
    ANONYMOUS

Who Ever hear on Sonday
Will Practis Playing at Ball
it May Be be Fore Monday
The Devil Will have you All.
    Inscription at Llanfair Discoed Church, South Wales

Let England boast Bath's crowded springs,
Llandrindod happier Cambria sings,
A greater, though a modern name,
by MERIT rising to its fame.
    Gentleman's Magazine
    Verse in praise of the 'new' spa town of Llandrindod Wells
    1748

That most magnificent badge of our subjection.
    THOMAS PENNANT
    A Tour in Wales, late 18th century
    Writing about Caernarfon Castle

One of the castles of Wales would contain all the castles ... in Scotland.
    DR SAMUEL JOHNSON
    Reputedly of Caernarfon Castle

"CARNARVON CASTLE, NORTH WALES."—A PAINTING BY EDWARD RICHARDSON.—IN THE EXHIBITION OF THE NEW SOCIETY OF PAINTERS IN WATER COLOURS.—PURCHASED BY HER MAJESTY.

The Welsh Quotation Book

Born in America, in Europe bred,
In Africa travell'd, and in Asia wed,
Where long he liv'd, and thriv'd; at London dead.
Much good, some ill, he did; so hope all's even,
And that his soul, thro' mercy's gone to heaven.
You that survive, and read, take care
For this most certain exit to prepare:
Where blest in peace, the actions of the just
Smell sweet, and blossom in the dust.
    Epitaph at Wrexham Church to Elihu Yale (d. 1721),
    Founder of Yale University

Under this yew tree
Buried would hee bee
For his father and hee
Planted this yew tree.
    Epitaph to Richard Jones (d. 1707) at Guilsfield, Mid
    Wales

The Welsh Quotation Book

[the liquid is] a powerful detergent, repelling, bracing, styptic, cicatrizing, anti-scorbutic and deobstruent medicine, as hath appeared by the notable cures they have effected ... in inveterate ulcers, the itch, mange, scab, tetterous eruptions, dysentries, internal haemorrages, in gleets, the fluor albus, and diorhea, in the worms, agues, dropsies and jaundice.

> DR JOHN RUTTY
> Speaking on the supposed medicinal qualities of the water from copper-rich Parys Mountain on Anglesey, 1760

Llandrindod Wells. The Famous Spa of Central Wales. The splendid, bracing air, and the saline, sulphur, magnesian and chalybeate waters are very efficacious in the treatment of gout, rheumatism, anaemia, neurasthenia, dyspepsia, diabetes, and liver affections. Complete system of baths; dowsing radiant heat bath; massage and nauheim treatment.

> An old advertising sign for Llandrindod Wells

Some of the more obstinate Criminals are punished by Suspension, but not by the Neck, as here in England, but by the Wrists, Thumb-rop'd together with String of Hay, and so fasten'd to a Peg; well! this is but the Beginning ... the Sting will follow: The offending Taphy thus dangling in the Air, the Beadle approaches with a stick imp'd with a Feather at one End, and tickles his Testicles; these softer Titillation engender some vibrations of the Body, and nimble Friskings, which are shrewdly chastis'd by a Cat-of-nine-tails.

For several Crimes they have various Punishments. That grand Enormity of Breaking-wind is chastised there as it is in England, that is, the Hand of Magistracy doth usually inflict a pretty lusty Cobbling, that is, for every Report of Loss of an Hair, though some that have been much addicted to that Infirmity, and therefore have been very guilty of a Stink, have endured the Cruelty of tormenting Fairies, that is, have been pinch'd into Manners, and a better Smell.

> JOHN TORBUCK
> *A Collection of Welsh Travels and Memoirs of Wales*
> 1738

No sooner was our supper dispatched, than Mrs Jones gave us notice, that at a neighbouring public-house the cottagers had met, and were dancing to the sound of the village harp. The idea of a *genuine Welsh Ball* pleased us highly ... The party ... consisted of twenty five or thirty ... animated by the tones of their favourite national instrument, and enlivened with the idea of the week's labours being terminated (for it was Saturday night), they entered into the business of the evening and exhibited a complete picture of perfect happiness ... men and women individually solicited us to dance. As the females were very handsome, it is most probable we should have accepted their offers, had there not been a powerful reason to prevent us – our complete inability to unravel the mazes of a Welsh dance.

> REVD RICHARD WARNER OF BATH
> *A Walk Through Wales in August 1797*

The Welsh Quotation Book

O! Could I make verses with humour and wit,
George Tennant, Esquire's great genius to fit;
From morn until even, I would sit down and tell,
And sing in the praise of Neath Junction Canal.

To his noble genius, great merit is due,
The increase of traffic, he daily pursue;
Employ to poor Labourers, it is known full well,
He gave them by making Neath Junction Canal.

Now this will improve the trade of the place,
I hope that the business will daily increase;
All sorts of provisions we shall have to sell,
Convey'd us in boats by Neath Junction Canal.

The work it is finish'd, and now is complete,
Without e'er a man with an accident meet;
Though there was great danger, yet nobody fell,
By building the Acquaduct of Neath Junction Canal.

The new Docks of Swansea will be very grand,
For floating the Vessels at their command,
Quite safe from all dangers when the high Tides do
　swell,
To take in the cargo for Neath Junction Canal.
　ELIZABETH DAVIES
　A few of her many verses in praise of the Neath
　Junction Canal, 1824

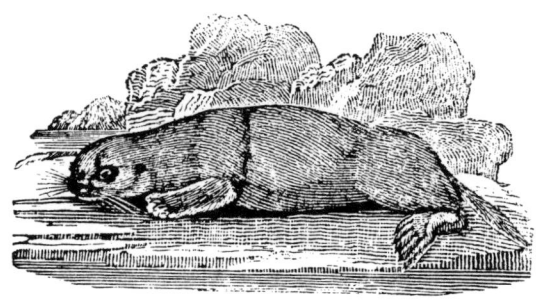

And oft, when gently moving by,
Have seen the trout, his vigor try,
To mount the fall, but all in vain;
The top he could never attain.

And in the deep, dark wave beneath,
How often lurk'd the hidden death;
With hairy coat, and aspect gaunt,
The otter makes that pool his haunt;
The finny tribes become his prey,
In caverns hid, from face of day.

Much alter'd now the scene appears;
And trade its busy form uprears;
Where silence reigned, now tumult rings;
So change is mark'd on human things.
    WILLIAM YOUNG
    Verses reflecting on the changed conditions in the
    Vale of Neath, 1835

... the clothes brush is a luxury as yet unknown in Llanrwst.
>   THOMAS BABINGTON MACAULAY
>   1821

London is chiefly supplied with slate from Bangor in Caernarfonshire.
>   W.T. BRANDE
>   *Outline of Geology*, 1817

There were 10 beds in three rooms, and the back premises are nearly as bad as those in any other part of the town. Fatal fever has prevailed here, and as many as 47 lodgers have been counted in the house.
>   Report to the General Board of Health on the
>   Borough of Bangor
>   1847

In following the sea-shore, we reached at Laugharne Castle the boundary line dividing Wales from the part of Pembrokeshire which has for centuries been dubbed 'Little England beyond Wales' ... for seven centuries this castle has marked the point beyond which the Welshman and the Fleming have refused to go, either in his way – never intermarrying, understanding not each other's language, and as completely divided in thought and feeling as if a high wall ran between them.
>   Observations of a Victorian traveller

The Welsh Quotation Book

Old Lady: In faith, for little England
You'ld venture an emballing: I my selfe
Would for *Carnarvanshire*.
   WILLIAM SHAKESPEARE
   Henry VIII

I would sooner go to hell than Wales.
   H.H. ASQUITH, MP
   1905

The coal valleys bear the marks, psychological as well as physical, of having been in the arena for a scramble by everybody, high and low, for quick money.
   THE TIMES
   1928

You the coalowners ... think you can suck the life-blood out of the colliers for ever. You have grown fat and prosperous; you own the big houses; you wear the finest clothes; your children are healthy and happy; yet you do not work ... Take heed, you men whose bodies are bloated by the life-blood of the poor, take heed before it is too late.
   WILLIAM PRICE
   1880

O what can you give me?
Say the sad bells of Rhymney.

Is there hope for the future?
Cry the brown bells of Merthyr.

24

The Welsh Quotation Book

Who made the mineowner?
Say the black bells of Rhondda.

And who robbed the miner?
Cry the grim bells of Blaina.

They will plunder willy-nilly,
Say the bells of Caerphilly.

They have fangs, they have teeth!
Shout the loud bells of Neath.

To the south, things are sullen,
Say the pink bells of Brecon.

Even God is uneasy,
Say the moist bells of Swansea.

Put the vandals in court!
Cry the bells of Newport.

All would be well if – if – if –
Say the green bells of Cardiff.

Why so worried, sister, why?
Sing the silver bells of Wye.
   IDRIS DAVIES
   Gwalia Deserta, 1938

The Welsh Quotation Book

Hereabouts, and for some miles to come, there is a degree of luxuriance in the valley, infinitely beyond what my entrance on this district led me to expect. The contrast of the meadows, rich and verdant, with mountains the most wild and romantic, surrounding them on every side, is in the highest degree picturesque.
>REVD BENJAMIN MALKIN
>Description of pre-industrial Rhondda

Revolutionary and riotous; religious and musical; sporting and artistic, coal-bearing Rhondda.
>JACK JONES
>*Rhondda Roundabout*, 1934

Merthyr Tydfil is remarkable for the number and extent of its iron-works ... Scarcely anything can be conceived more awfully grand than the descent, on a dark night, into the Vale of Merthyr Tydfil ... where on a sudden the traveller beholds, as it were, numberless volcanoes breathing out their undulating pillars of flame and smoke.
>MARQUESS OF BUTE
>1833

God Forgive Me
>Inscription on tomb of 19th-century Merthyr Tydfil ironmaster Robert Crawshay

The Welsh Quotation Book

I can hardly expect credence for such facts as the following, yet it is perfectly free from exaggeration. I saw a young woman filling her pitcher from a little stream of water gushing from a cinder heap the surface of which was so thickly studded with alvine deposits that it was difficult to pass without treading on them, in some of which I saw intestine worms, and the rain then falling was washing the feculent matter into the water which the girl was filling into her pitcher, no doubt for domestic use.

> A visitor to Merthyr Tydfil in the early days of the industrial revolution

'Tis like a vision of Hell, and will never leave me, that of these poor creatures broiling, or in sweat and dirt, amid their furnaces, pits, and rolling mills.

> THOMAS CARLYLE
> Description of 19th-century Merthyr Tydfil

The men employed at these works are too much addicted to drinking; but in other respects no great immoralities are to be found among them; far less indeed than might have been expected, from the tide of dissoluteness which is usually found to flow in upon a place, from the rapid increase of vulgar population.

> Description of workers at Merthyr Tydfil's ironworks
> Early 19th century

The Welsh Quotation Book

Merthyr was a great place for a boy to grow up I think. It was a sad town of course, in the Twenties and Thirties, but wonderful for boys. It was full of great characters. Children were valued in that place for some odd reason ... Around the town it was incredibly beautiful. And so I knew early on. I had concrete evidence early on of the difference between the ideal and the hellish.
    LESLIE NORRIS
    Recalling his memories of Merthyr Tydfil, 1983

We went from end to end of the Midlands, through miles of built-up areas ... This made me realise how different 'industrial' South Wales is from that, especially Merthyr up there are the end of the valley with ... the Beacons only a Mabinogion-character's stone's throw away. There's no comparison. We were brought up in Arcady compared with some of those poor little Midlanders.
    GLYN JONES
    1971

Unemployment was the evil that drove nearly half-a-million of our people from Wales between the two wars. It is the evil that breaks up our homes and our Welsh communities, and destroys our culture and our sense of nationhood.
    S.O. DAVIES, MP
    1949

Anybody could find a job in Maerdy in those days. They never turned anyone away. If a man had only one arm or one leg, they'd find some work for him in the colliery.
    Recollections of a miner, late 19th century

The first thing I saw was the slag heap.

Big it had grown, and long, and black, without life or sign, lying along the bottom of the Valley on both sides of the river. The green grass, and the reeds and the flowers, all had gone, crushed beneath it. And every minute the burden grew, as cage after cage screeched along the cables from the pit, bumped to a stop at the tipping pier, and emptied dusty loads on to the ridged, black, dirty back.

On our side of the Valley the heap reached to the front garden walls of the bottom row of houses, and children from them were playing up and down the black slopes, screaming and shouting, laughing in fun ... and all the time I was watching, the cable screeched and the cages tipped. From the Britannia pit came a call on the hooter as the cages came up, as though to remind the Valley to be ready for more filth as the work went on and on, year in and year out.
    RICHARD LLEWELYN
    How Green Was My Valley, 1939

The Welsh Quotation Book

I remember sitting in the Palladium in Aberdare in the late sixties watching a re-run of *How Green Was My Valley* and thinking for the first time, this is a film extolling the virtues of scabs, full of Welshmen with Irish accents, and it's absolute nonsense; yet I looked around and the entire audience had their eyes filled with tears – in one of the most left-wing constituencies in Britain.
    KIM HOWELLS, MP
    Planet, 1985

What he did know was that the hardest working men in the world were the worst paid, and that men going half a mile down to cut coal often had nothing better for their tommy tins than bread and jam, and that butterless.
    GWYN JONES
    Times Like These, 1936

Twenty-six per cent of Welshman unemployed. Bread is dearer. England spends £1,500 million on War.
    WELSH LITERARY JOURNAL
    1937

The Welsh Quotation Book

Something must be done.
> EDWARD, PRINCE OF WALES
> During a visit to Merthyr Tydfil, 1936

These valleys are not all colliery-sidings and slag-heaps and crooked streets. There are pleasant places among the hillsides, and there is some variety of scenery ... Even the old slag-heaps themselves are more than mere slag-heaps to some of us. They are for ever associated with generations of our people who gave so much of their blood and sweat in the years gone by.
> IDRIS DAVIES
> 1943

Before this event we stand breathless. Our eyes speak, our thoughts rage, but our tongues have momentarily given up the ghost of immemorial grievance. No touch of the whip has hurt quite like this.
> GWYN THOMAS
> Speaking of the Aberfan disaster, 1966

Greed to mine as much coal for our energy needs as we could, without caring too much about the waste products – and it occurred to me in this year of Chernobyl, when who knows how many innocent people will again perish as a result of man's search for energy, that the lesson of Aberfan is that in our pursuit for warmth and heat and light we still owe a duty of care to each other, and between communities, and between nations.
> VINCENT KANE
> The broadcaster speaking in 1986, twenty years after the Aberfan disaster

The Welsh Quotation Book

The mining valleys of the South are full of life, eager, vivid, mercurial and yet determined, a life somehow Latin in quickness. The North is quieter, slower in pulse, less accustomed to living in large aggregations, less penetrated by different nationalities.
>   WYN GRIFFITH
>   *The Welsh*, 1950

For those wishing to commit sin, a mining village is the hardest terrain. An extra-mural sinner in that setting is the object of more intense research than atomic energy or the toxic reach of mercury.
>   GWYN THOMAS
>   *Western Mail*

Well, I started in January 1890. I worked January, February and March and the Act came into force that said you couldn't work underground until you was twelve. Well, I wasn't eleven. There was seventeen of us turned back at the Drift, Derlwyn Drift, turned back you know. I went back to school for twelve months, one half day I missed in that twelve months. I realised that school was easier than working underground, six bob a week and half of that going in oil to fill your lamp ... we never got much. Now I married on June 1st, 1903, I was stoking then. Eighty-four hours a week for twenty-nine and six. Now you tell the teenagers that today, they won't bloody believe you.
>   WILLIAM HARRIES
>   An ex-miner from Bargoed speaking in 1970; quoted in *Coalface* (1982) by Richard Keen

I never really got over leaving Aberaman, and I know a great many other Welshmen who never recovered that sense of living in an intimate community which every Welsh valley provides, that concern about one another, a bit too nosey at times, you may say, curiosity, inquisitiveness rather than concern.
    KENNETH HARRIS
    1956

'Cos it's hard, Duw it's hard,
It's harder than they will ever know,
And it's they must take the blame,
The price of coal's the same,
But the pit-head baths is a supermarket now.
    MAX BOYCE
    Duw it's Hard, 1974

The Welsh Quotation Book

Is Wales becoming nothing more than a nation of museum attendants? My Orwellian nightmare is a big black sign at the Severn Bridge: 'You are now entering a protected industrial relic. Pay £5 to view this disappearing society.'
>HYWEL FRANCIS
>*Arcade*, 1981

I just hope we're not going to become a kind of ossified backwater ... or an appendage to England, a tourist place with industrial museums the biggest growth industry. But there's something, a kind of magic, that keeps us here, I suppose, though I don't know what it is, mind.
>KIM HOWELLS, MP
>1985

I do not easily believe in patriotism, in times of peace or war, or the result of intoxication or an article in a newspaper, unless I am in Wales.
>EDWARD THOMAS (1878–1917)

It is easy to love Wales when you are far away from it making a fortune in England.
>W.J. GRUFFYDD
>*Y Llenor*, 1931

Wales suffers greatly from stereotypes, often self-inflicted.
>   JAN MORRIS
>   1980

The liking of Welshmen for Welshmen in very strong, and that not only when they meet on foreign soil, as in London, but in their own land. They do not, I suppose, love their neighbours more than other men do, but when they meet a fellow-countryman for the first time they seem to have a kind of surprise and joy, in spite of the commonness of such meetings. They do not acquiesce in the fact that the man they shake hands with is of their race, as the English do. They converse readily in trains: they are all of one family, and indeed if you are Welsh, not only can you not avoid meeting relatives, but you do not wish to.
>   EDWARD THOMAS
>   *Wales*, 1905

I am only a bit of a Welshman in an office in London.
>   DAVID LLOYD GEORGE, MP
>   1915

   What is life if, full of care
   We have no time to stand and stare.
>   W.H. DAVIES
>   1911

The Welsh Quotation Book

When it pleases him – and it quite frequently does please him – Mr Lloyd George can be very proud of his Welshness.
    T.W.H. CROSLAND
    Taffy was a Welshman, 1912

Every summer, whatever the weather, streams of South Wales workers and their children leave their valleyed prisons and flow by bus, charabanc and train to the nearest seaside place some twenty or forty miles away.
    LEWIS JONES
    1935

  Let's go to Barry Island, Maggie fach,
  And give the kids one day by the sea.
    IDRIS DAVIES
    1943

Until I was eighteen I suppose I had hardly ever left Wales; and I remember that my strongest desire was to leave it for what I imagined to be the less constricted, less narrow, less puritanical life of other countries. Since then I have not lived in Wales except for very brief periods. I have lived in England and abroad, and I confess that by now I am much fonder of my country than before; and my people seem to me to possess more of those qualities I admire, of passion, intelligence, individualism, and of natural devotion to culture than almost any other I have known.
    GORONWY REES
    1938

The Welsh Quotation Book

This life in London – what a waste
Of time and comfort, in this place;
With all its noise, and nothing seen
But what is stone or human face.
Twigs thin and bare, like sparrows' legs.
Yet back to Nature I must go –
To see the thin, mosquito flakes
Grow into moths of plumper snow.

What is this life, if, like bad clocks,
We keep no time and are but going;
What is my breath worth when I hear
A hundred horns and whistles blowing;
The rushing cars that crunch their way,
Still followed by the heavy carts;
Till I, with all my senses stunned,
Am deafened to my very thoughts?
    W.H. DAVIES (1871–1940)
    Traffic

One learns in London to look almost with terror at the great machine-made civilisation rampant there; with all its selfishness, cruelty and materialism ... and to look back to Wales, its green pastures and pleasant waters, its mountains and its simpler life with a great sense of relief.
    ERNEST RHYS (1859–1946)

I should like to record that my simple, narrow Welsh mind is completely puzzled to understand how writing in English has any connection with Welsh literature or culture.
    TOM H. RICHARDS
    Western Mail, 1939

The Welsh Quotation Book

These first months in the autumn of 1942, I loathed the fogs, London's apparent offhandedness. I longed for the provincial friendliness of Welsh people. I wanted to hear a bit of Welsh spoken, or, at least, the accented sing-song voices that I knew so well with all their cosmic portentousness.
    DANNIE ABSE
    Poet in the Family, 1974

The girl who goes to England to work in an arms factory at the government's orders is sure to get into trouble ... if she had stayed at home, serving in a café in Aber-rheidol, she would probably have become a vicar's wife.
    Criticism of D.J. Williams's story, *Ceinwen*, 1949

England includes Wales, but does not include Scotland.
    SIR DONALD SOMERVILLE
    1949

Being Jewish in a Welsh community is being as it were a minority within a minority ... I'm a Welsh Jew or Jewish Welshman like ... Aneurin Levy who lives somewhere between Ystlafera and Ystrad Mynach, and like Llewellyn ap Goldstein who owns a sweet shop not far from Abercwmboi.
    DANNIE ABSE
    From a 1955 broadcast

When you can see the coast of Devon from Swansea, it's going to rain; when you can't, it's already raining.
    ANONYMOUS

Year after year I have felt that only friends could bring me again to Swansea. But the town is a dirty witch. You must hate or love her, and I both love and hate her ...
EDWARD THOMAS
Early 20th century

This town has got as many layers as an onion, and each one reduces you to tears.
DYLAN THOMAS
On his birthplace, Swansea

Old Swansea was never planned. It was doodled over the landscape.
WYNFORD VAUGHAN-THOMAS
Trust to Talk, 1980

I was born in a large Welsh industrial town at the beginning of the Great War: an ugly, lovely town (or so it was, and is, to me), crawling, sprawling, slummed, unplanned, jerry-villa'd, and smug-suburbed by the side of a long and splendid-curving shore ... This sea town was my world; outside, a *strange* Wales, coal-pitted, mountained, river run, full, so far as I knew, of choirs and sheep and story-book tall hats, moved about its business which was none of mine ...
DYLAN THOMAS
Reminiscences of Childhood

The Welsh Quotation Book

To begin at the beginning:
It is spring, moonless night in the small town, starless and bible-black, the cobblestreets silent and the hunched, courters'-and-rabbits' wood limping invisible down the sloeback, slow, black, crowblack, fishingboat-bobbing sea. The houses are blind as moles (though moles see fine to-night in the snouting, velvet dingles) or blind as Captain Cat there in the muffled middle by the pump and the town clock, the shops in mourning, the Welfare Hall in widows' weeds. And all the people of the lulled and dumbfounded town are sleeping now.
    DYLAN THOMAS
    The opening passage of *Under Milk Wood*

It was my thirtieth year to heaven
Woke to my hearing from harbour and neighbour wood
And the mussel pooled and the heron
Priested shore
The morning beckon
With water praying and call of seagull and rook
And the knock of sailing boats on the net webbed wall
Myself to set foot
That second
In the still sleeping town and set forth.
    DYLAN THOMAS
    Opening lines of *Poem in October*

The Welsh Quotation Book

One: I am a Welshman; two: I am a drunkard; three: I am a lover of the human race, especially of women.
    DYLAN THOMAS

He had harvested the poem's familiar tips
Till his two lips were red;
Truth on the grapes till, drunken,
He fell dead, widowed the wine.
    EUROS BOWEN
    Dylan Thomas

Dylan Thomas – in so far as one can tell this sort of thing – was a writer of enormous natural talent – whatever that means – and I think he perverted it. It's a perilous thing to say and a very arrogant thing to say but I think his view of what poetry is and ought to be doing was a dangerous one; in a way, a ridiculous one. He tried to reduce everything to words on the page and, as far as possible, to forget what they meant or what they meant outside poetry.
    KINGSLEY AMIS
    On Dylan Thomas, 1987

Everything else didn't matter, of course. I mean bills, money, appointments, they were of no importance whatever compared with the word, but when it was the matter of the word then he was as conscientious as a bank clerk.
    DOUGLAS CLEVERDON
    On Dylan Thomas, 1983

The Welsh Quotation Book

... I worshipped Dylan, I thought he was a great poet and a great reader. I thought he was a lovely man and when he died, I wept ... if ever I thought a man had a touch of divinity it was Dylan.
JOHN ARLOTT
On Dylan Thomas, 1983

I loved a man whose name was Tom
He was strong as a bear and two yards long
I loved a man whose name was Dick
He was big as a barrel and three feet thick
And I loved a man whose name was Harry
Six feet tall and sweet as a cherry
But the one I loved best awake or asleep
Was little Willy Wee and he's six feet deep.
DYLAN THOMAS
Polly Garter in *Under Milk Wood*

'Wales' and the 'Welsh' are disparaging terms for a country, a people and its language. The words derive from an ancient Germanic word *wealas* 'foreigner', applied by the incoming Anglo-Saxons to the resident British who were henceforth strangers in their own land.
VICTOR STEVENSON
Words, 1983

It is to be observed that the British language is more delicate and richer in north Wales, that country being less intermixed with foreigners.
GIRALDUS CAMBRENSIS (GERALD OF WALES)
Description of Wales, 12th century

The Welsh Quotation Book

Ability in English I never had,
Neither knew phrases of passionate French:
A stranger and foolish, when I've asked questions
It turned out crooked – I spoke North Welsh!

On a wave may God's son grant us our wish
And out from amongst them readily bring us
To a Wales made one, content and fair,
To a prince throned, laden nobly with gifts,
To the lord of Dinorwig's bright citadel land,
To the country of Dafydd, where Welsh freely flows!
   DAFYDD BENFRAS
   From Exile, 13th century

It is very strange to me that the Welsh are so uncaring towards me [the Welsh language] and I so useless to them, especially ... as I am so abundant in letters, so rich in words, so ancient in my origins.
   GRUFFYDD ROBERT
   16th century

Gwlad, gwlad, pleidiol wyf i'm gwlad!
Tra mor yn fur i'r bur hoff bau
O bydded i'r hen iaith barhau!

Home, home, true am I to home,
While seas secure the land so pure,
Oh may the old language endure.
   HEN WLAD FY NHADAU (THE LAND OF MY FATHERS)
   Chorus of Wales's national anthem

The Welsh Quotation Book

The sound of Welsh, in a continued discourse, is not unpleasant.
> DR SAMUEL JOHNSON
> *The Diary of a Journey Through North Wales in 1774*

The Celt goes talking from Llanberis to Kirkwall,
but the English, ah the English, don't say a word at all!
> RUDYARD KIPLING

Their native gibberish is usually prattled throughout the whole of Taphydom except in their market towns ...
> WILLIAM RICHARDS
> 17th century

The Welsh language is the curse of Wales. Its prevalence and the ignorance of English have excluded and even now exclude the Welsh people from civilization, the improvement and the material prosperity of their English neighbours. Their antiquated and semi-barbarous language, in short, shrouds them in darkness ... For all purposes, Welsh is a dead language.
> THE TIMES
> 1866

... I soon gave up trying to learn Welsh. But the idea of Wales and the idea of Welsh mythology went drumming on like an incantation through my tantalized soul.
> JOHN COWPER POWYS
> *Autobiography*, 1934

... like a growing child I am now trying to master a new language – the Welsh language. I learn Welsh not only in order to get to know the riches of Welsh literature ... but in order to come nearer to the soul of the Welsh.
>   KATE BOSSE-GRIFFITHS
>   1942

Give up, Taffy. It's a dead language. Petrol pump is pwmp petrol, atomic bomb is bom atomig, a tin of salmon is tun o samwn. And what is the Welsh word for 'bingo'? Ha ha.
>   T. GLYNNE DAVIES
>   1966

To a Welshman a fence is for leaning on for a chat; to an Englishman it is to ensure privacy.
>   TREVOR FISHLOCK
>   *Talking of Wales*, 1976

They went outside and stood where a sign used to say Taxi and now said Taxi/Tacsi for the benefit of Welsh people who had never seen a letter x before.
>   KINGSLEY AMIS
>   *The Old Devils*, 1986

It has often struck me that a world-weary man ... could do no better than revolve amongst these modest inns in the five northern Welsh counties ... Happier life I cannot imagine than this vagrancy, if the weather were but tolerable.
>   THOMAS DE QUINCEY
>   *The Confessions of an English Opium Eater*, 1821

The rain grew heavier.
>	REVD FRANCIS KILVERT
>	Diary entry after climbing Cader Idris above
>	Dolgellau, 13 June 1871

Rainwater streamed down the walls of the 'Harp'. It had rained for a week. There was nothing of the many things I could feel around me in the dark that was not soaked. I wore a waterproof jacket. That jacket was thick and good. It had belonged to an uncle of mine. I took it from his house without telling anybody, just after he died. The rain did not bother him any more. It bothered me.
>	GWYN THOMAS
>	Writing about the rain in the South Wales valleys in *Oscar*

I am getting almost fond of the rain. You have to admire its persistence. Even in the middle of the night when there's no one around to watch it comes doggedly down, and by day when it isn't actually pouring it is flirting with the idea of doing so, drizzling delicately down the backs of people's collars and into the tops of their wellies. I have isolated three of its modes – spitting, pouring and absolutely pissing down – and I'm sure if I studied it closely I would discern more.
>	ALICE THOMAS ELLIS
>	Writing about the rain in North Wales in *Home Life*

The Welsh Quotation Book

Welsh rain ... it descends with the enthusiasm of someone breaking bad news ... It runs round corners with the wind. It finds its way up your sleeves and down your neck ... rain in Wales can seem directed by some malignant producer, someone bent on drowning the earth and wiping from the mind of man all memory of dry places.
> H.V. MORTON
> *In Search of Wales*, 1932

... the wildest and most terrifying region in all Wales. For its mountains are very high and inaccessible, with crags as sharply pointed as the defences of a fortress. Nor are these mountains widely spaced out, but all jumbled so closely together that shepherds can exchange comments or abuse from neighbouring peaks.
> GIRALDUS CAMBRENSIS (GERALD OF WALES)
> *Journey through Wales*, 12th century
> Description of Snowdonia

As Dyfed ... is the fairest of all the lands of Wales, as Pembrokeshire is the fairest part of Dyfed, and this spot the fairest of Pembroke, it follows that Manorbier is the sweetest spot in Wales.
> GIRALDUS CAMBRENSIS (GERALD OF WALES)
> *Journey through Wales*, 12th century
> Of his birthplace

The Welsh Quotation Book

Pistyll Rhaeadr and Wrexham Steeple,
Snowdon's mountain, without its people;
Overton Yewtrees, Saint Winifred's Wells,
Llangollen Bridge and Gresford Bells.
    THE TRADITIONAL 'SEVEN WONDERS OF WALES'

The Vale of Festiniog is the perfectly beautiful of all we have seen. With the woman one loves, with the friend of one's heart and a study of books, one might pass an age in this vale and think it a day.
    LORD LYTTLETON
    18th century

By fair Festiniog, mid the Northern Hills,
The vales are full of beauty, and the heights,
Thin set with mountain sheep, show statelier far
Than in the tamer South.
    SIR LEWIS MORRIS,
    Lyn y Morwynion, 1887

I shall here conclude my remarks on this Principality by observing that its natural beauties cannot be sufficiently revered and admired; nor can the bad accommodation at most of the receptacles for the traveller, and the insolence and inattention of the proprietors, joined to the filthiness of their attendants, be sufficiently censured.
    HENRY WIGSTEAD
    A Tour of North and South Wales in the year 1797

The Welsh Quotation Book

If you ever go to Dolgelley,
Don't stay at the Lion Hotel,
There's nothing to put in your belly,
And no one to answer the bell.
   ANONYMOUS
   18th century

As we entered Dolgelly the old man said, 'You're a splendid walker, Sir', a compliment which procured him a glass of brandy and water.
   REVD FRANCIS KILVERT
   Kilvert's Diary, 1870–79

... we sometimes see these Mountains rising up at once from the lowest Valleys to the highest Summits, which makes the Height look horrid and frightful, *even worse* than those Mountains Abroad.
   DANIEL DEFOE
   A Tour through the Whole Island of Britain, 1724
   On the Brecon Beacons

Brecknockshire is a meer inland county, as Radnor is; the English jestingly (and I think not very improperly) call it Breakneckshire: 'Tis mountainous to an extremity, except on the side of Radnor, where it is somewhat more low and level.
   DANIEL DEFOE
   A Tour through the Whole Island of Britain, 1724

The Welsh Quotation Book

This combination of mountainous scenery is truly sublime and surpasses any thing I have seen.
>J.M.W. TURNER
>*Diary of a Tour in Part of Wales*, 1792

Leave to Robert Browning
Beggars, fleas and vines;
Leave to squeamish Ruskin
Popish Apennines,
Dirty stones of Venice
And his gas-lamps seven;
We've the stones of Snowdon
And the lamps of heaven.
>CHARLES KINGSLEY
>*The Invitation*
>In a letter to Thomas Hughes, 1856

How awful in the silence of the waste,
Where nature lifts her mountains to the sky.
Majestic solitude, behold the tower
Where hopeless OWEN, long imprisoned, pin'd
And wrung his hands for liberty in vain.
>J.M.W. TURNER
>Verse to accompany his painting of Dolbadarn Castle, Snowdonia, in the catalogue of an exhibition, 1800

Steal, if possible, my revered friend, one summer from the cold hurry of business, and come to Wales.
>PERCY BYSSHE SHELLEY
>1812

The Welsh Quotation Book

It was last summer on a tour in Wales:
Old James was with me: we that day had been
Up Snowdon; and I wished for Leonard there,
As found him in Llanberis; then we crost
Between the lakes, and clambered half way up
The counter side ...
... and, high above, I heard them blast
Snowdon Mountain, ravenous snow
melted, windy often.
In distress best is a relation.
   THOMAS PENNANT
   A Tour in Wales
   Late 18th century

In one of these excursions, travelling then
Through Wales on foot, and with a youthful Friend,
I left Bethkelet's huts at couching-time,
And westward took my way to see the sun
Rise from the top of Snowdon. Having reach'd
The Cottage at the Mountain's foot, we there
Rouz'd up the Shepherd, who by ancient right
Of office is the Stranger's usual guide;
And after short refreshment sallied forth.
   WILLIAM WORDSWORTH
   Opening lines of Book 13 of *The Prelude*

I have walked thrice up Snowdon, which I found very much easier to accomplish than walking on level ground.
   ALFRED, LORD TENNYSON
   1844

The Welsh Quotation Book

The steep slate quarry, and the great echo flap
And buffet round the hills from bluff to bluff.
    ALFRED, LORD TENNYSON
    The Golden Years

And they went up Snowdon, too, and saw little beside fifty fog-blinded tourists, five-and-twenty dripping ponies, and five hundred empty porter bottles; wherefrom they returned, as do many, disgusted, and with great colds in their heads.
    CHARLES KINGSLEY
    Two Years Ago, 1857

I have ... been made sensible by Wordsworth of one grievous defect in the structure of the Welsh valleys; too generally they take the *basin* shape – the level area at their foot does not detach itself with sufficient precision from the declivities that surround them.
    THOMAS DE QUINCEY
    Autobiography, 1834–53

It was a pretty sight to see the group of ladies with their fresh light dresses moving up and down the long green meadow ... All through the hot burning afternoon how pleasant sounded the cool rush and roar of the Wye over its rapids and rocks at the end of the meadow.
    REVD FRANCIS KILVERT
    Kilvert's Diary, 1870–79

The Welsh Quotation Book

… the Cockney is a more dangerous enemy than ever was Saxon or Norman. We have to encounter all kinds of saucy cosmopolitanism and resist all kinds of cheap commercial bribes – all those things in short that seek to destroy the national sentiment, and make Wales into a London suburb, and Snowdon – the sacred mountain of our fathers – into a railway station.
>ERNEST RHYS (1859–1946)
>At the time of the opening of the Snowdon Mountain Railway

While the English roads are crowded with travelling parties of pleasure, the Welsh are so rarely visited that the author did not meet with a single party during his six weeks journey in Wales.
>HENRY PENRUDDOCKE WYNDHAM
>*A Gentleman's Tour through Monmouthshire and Wales*, 1797

On our way we stopped in Monmouthshire, my old home. I found it, I am glad to say not farther from heaven than when I was a boy, but rather nearer to it: quite wonderful, enchanting and enchanting.
>ARTHUR MACHEN (1863–1947)

I shall always esteem it as the greatest piece of fortune that has fallen upon me that I was born in that noble, fallen Caerleon-on-Usk in the heart of Gwent.
>ARTHUR MACHEN
>*Far Off Things*, 1922

The Welsh Quotation Book

Can I forget the sweet days that have been,
When poetry first began to warm my blood;
When from the hills of Gwent I saw the earth
Burned into two by Severn's silver flood:

When I would go alone at night to see
The moonlight, like a big white butterfly,
Dreaming on that old castle near Caerleon,
While at its side the Usk went softly by:

When I would stare at lovely clouds in Heaven,
Or watch them when reported by deep streams;
When feeling pressed like thunder, but would not
Break into that grand music of my dreams?

Can I forget the sweet days that have been,
The villages so green I have been in;
Llantarnam, Magor, Malpas and Llanwern,
Liswery, old Caerleon, and Alteryn?

Can I forget the banks of Malpas Brook,
Or Ebbw's voice in such a wild delight,
As on he dashed with pebbles in his throat,
Gurgling towards the sea with all his might?

Ah, when I see a leafy village now,
I sigh and ask it for Llantarnam's green;
I ask each river where is Ebbw's voice –
In memory of the sweet days that have been.
   W.H. DAVIES (1871–1940)
   Days That Have Been

The last cloud and mist rolled away over the mountain tops and the mountains stood up in the clear blue heven, a long rampart line of dazzling glittering snow ... I stood rooted to the ground, struck with amazement and overwhelmed at the extraordinary splendour of this marvellous spectacle. I never saw anything to equal it I think, even among the high Alps.
    REVD FRANCIS KILVERT
    Diary entry describing the Black Mountains

The salmon's no traitor – from his adventure
He goes back home;
When you're tired of sampling towns
It's pleasant to look homeward.
    LLAWDDEN
    Going Home

Nature and Time are against us now:
no more we leap up the river like salmon,
nor dive through its fishy holes
sliding along its summer corridor
with all the water from Wales ...
    MARGIAD EVANS (1909–58)

O Wales of the dark blue marshland and rocks,
The rearing place of independence of mind,
Your firmness remains above the chaos
From age to age.
    WALDO WILLIAMS (1904–71)

I think most Welshmen love Wales more than most Englishmen love England.
    TREVOR FISHLOCK
    Wales and the Welsh, 1972

The countryside is so beautiful ... You vant to put it on the map, make it go, like the Swiss do. No-body knows about it! Vales for the Velsh. I believe in Vales for the Velsh ... but you can have too much Vales for the Velsh.
    GERAINT GOODWIN
    Businessman Mr Birbaum in *The Heyday in the Blood*, 1936

The Welsh Quotation Book

Lovely the woods, waters, meadows, combes, vales,
All the air things wear that built this world of Wales.
   GERARD MANLEY HOPKINS (1844–89)
   In the Valley of the Elwy

About a mile above Llanthony we descried the Abbey ruins, the dim grey pile of building in the vale below standing by the little riverside among its brilliant green meadow. What was our horror on entering the enclosure to see two tourists with staves and shoulder belts all complete postured among the ruins in an attitude of admiration, one of them of course discoursing learnedly to his gaping companion and pointing out objects of interest with his stick. If there is one thing more hateful than another it is being told what to admire and having objects pointed out to one with a stick. Of all noxious animals too the most noxious is a tourist. And of all tourists the most vulgar, illbred, offensive and loathsome is the British tourist.
   REVD FRANCIS KILVERT
   Kilvert's Diary, 1870–79

The staid respectability of the architecture ... is that of middle life, and seems to scorn the novelties which find favour in the newer and more frivolous watering places.
   JOHN EDWARD LLOYD
   Description of late 19th-century Aberystwyth

In the way of amusement, Aberystwyth does not try to compete with such boisterous places as Blackpool or Douglas ... Sir Astley Cooper, and other fashionable physicians in the old coaching days, proclaimed the wonderful results of a short residence in this the 'Biarritz of Wales' ...
>   *Picturesque Wales*
>   Description in 1920s travel book

A visit to the establishment – quite recently – made it apparent that its patrons move in the highest society ... No member of the fair sex can have any excuse for remaining ill-dressed after examining the beautiful models which we have seen.
>   *Picturesque Wales*
>   Advertisement for Paris House Fashion Emporium, Aberystwyth

The inaccessibility of Aberystwyth to the outside world must be accepted as a dispensation of Providence. Such a town deserves to be isolated.
>   THOMAS DAVIES
>   1884

There is something sadistic about a Sunday in Aberystwyth.
>   RHYS DAVIES
>   *My Wales*, 1937

The Welsh Quotation Book

We took the side road through the meadows then the road to Llyn Ogwen, and we said what we always say – that the extraordinary thing about this part of Wales is how the landscape changes completely every five miles or so, from pastoral calm to frightening bleakness and back again. As we approached Bethesda the air was unusually clear and the sun bright, and the mountains looked oddly one-dimensional like a backdrop. They have made a number of films round here pretending that it's India or China, but today for some reason it felt exactly like the Wild West, and as we bowled along the valley bottom we thought how utterly detestable it would be if we were being pursued by Red Indians and how fortunate we were to be threatened by nothing more annoying than the Jehovah's Witnesses who have suddenly appeared in droves in Pen-y-Bont Fawr.
    ALICE THOMAS ELLIS
    Home Life

When Merlin's Oak shall tumble down,
then shall fall Carmarthen town.
    Traditional prophecy concerning an ancient oak
    which has now been removed

Carmarthen, a large Town, all white-washed – the Roofs of the Houses all white-washed! a great Town in a Confectioner's shop, on Twelfth cake Day or a huge Show piece at a distance.
    S.T. COLERIDGE
    Letter to Mrs S.T. Coleridge, 16 November 1802

The Welsh Quotation Book

The Welsh are quite incapable of directing one anywhere. Mention a place a mile from their home and perhaps they know it; two miles away and they have heard of it in myth and legend; three miles and it might as well have been Dar-es-Salaam. But lacking in any notion of honesty, and desiring to seem helpful and wise, they invent elaborate directions for getting there ... They are poets and romantics and they have fertile imaginations; their tongues run away with them and consequently they send the unfortunate traveller about ten miles out of his way.
    MOORE
    Tramping Through Wales, 1931

The wild Wales described by nineteenth-century travellers and painters is still there all right; smaller, beleaguered, but surviving. I walked in some of the finest mountain country anywhere in the world and, in the country, heard more Welsh spoken than English. There is still wilderness and its antiquity and beauty remain endlessly impressive.
    TREVOR FISHLOCK
    Talking of Wales, 1976

... in natural terms it is a wonderfully well-proportioned country. Nothing is too big, nothing lasts too long, and there is perpetual variety.
    JAN MORRIS
    1984

The Welsh Quotation Book

The colour of the snooker table fascinates me. Having an allergy to lawn mowers, I find a deep calm in the sight of anything green that doesn't grow.
    GWYN THOMAS
    Western Mail

Though it appear a little out of fashion,
There is much care and valour in this Welshman.
    WILLIAM SHAKESPEARE
    The king's description of Fluellyn, *Henry V*

The Welsh are the Irish who couldn't swim.
    ANONYMOUS

We were more especially pleased with the female part of the company. A round, candid, open countenance, illuminated by a brilliant complexion, dark eyes, and teeth of dazzling whiteness, and a certain indescribable *naiveté*, (which happily blends archness and simplicity, a great deal of intelligence, with an equal share of modesty) give an air peculiarly agreeable and characteristical to the Welsh girls. Some degree of whimsicality arose from our questioning these fair market women relative to the prices of the various articles they sold (of which we wished to acquire an accurate idea) and the difficulty that attended our being intelligible to each other. The guttural sounds they uttered (which even the voice and manner of a Welsh girl cannot render pleasing or harmonious) were totally thrown away upon our ignorance; whilst the roughnesses and sibilisms of our own Saxon dialect only excited an arch laugh from these virgin descendants of the ancient Britons.
    REVD RICHARD WARNER OF BATH
    A Walk Through Wales in August 1797
    At Abergavenny market

A country of small farmers surely breeds an admirable race of women! ... They may have to work hard, and even live hard, but they have independence, at any rate, and a settled home, and a good position in the rustic democracy, and, as long as the rent is paid, may reasonably count, in Wales, on seeing their home remain indefinitely in the family, and their children's children succeed them. As to the maidens of North Wales, they show beyond doubt a high average of comeliness.
    ARTHUR BRADLEY
    Highways and Byways in North Wales, 1898

The want of chastity is the besetting evil of this country ...
   ANONYMOUS
   19th century

... if drunkenness, idleness, mischief and revenge are the principal characteristics of the savage state, what nation, I will not say in Europe, but the world, is so singularly tattooed with them than the Welsh? ... I shall never cease to wish that Julius Caesar had utterly exterminated the whole race of Britons. I am convinced that they are as irreclaimable as Gypsies or Malays.
   WALTER SAVAGE LANDOR
   Comments by the poet and self-styled Lord of the Manor at Llanthony in the early 19th century, whose short-lived tenure ended in deserved disaster

The Welsh Quotation Book

In our own prosaic days we fail to estimate the awful power once wielded by the poet. In old days the poet was a priest, the priest a poet; the poet was a soldier, and the soldier was a poet. Poetry was not incompatible with the dignity of the soldier, or the sanctity of the priest. Tuning his song to the wild notes of his harp, the Welsh bard kindled the enthusiasm of his countrymen.

But one cannot help appreciating the genius of those old Welsh Princes who knew nothing of 'natural boundaries', and were ready to shed their blood, and the blood of their children, to preserve intact the legacy of their fathers. Now-a-days the animosity has died out – we are *British* – we belong to one another – our races have commingled; and whether we meet as host and tourist on the banks of a Welsh river, or whether we fight side by side in a foreign campaign, our cause, our hopes – our nationality is identical.

    JOHN TILLOTSON
    Picturesque Scenery in Wales, 1860

We like the bonny Scotsman with his tartan and his tam,
We also like the Yankee from the land of Uncle Sam.
But when it comes to Birmingham we couldn't give a Dam
And we just don't like the Sais.
    WELSH FOLK SONG
    Sais means English

The Welsh population of Merthyr is gathered in large part from the mountains and wildish valleys hereabouts, and includes some specimens of the race who (as the phrase goes) have no English, with a very large number of specimens who have but little and utter it brokenly. Those of the lower class who can read – and almost all Welshmen, however poor and primitive, can read – generally read Welsh only; and in that respect, as indeed in most respects, are far in advance of Englishmen of the same state in life, who often can read nothing. To hear a poor and grimy Welshman, who looks as if he might not have a thought above bread and beer, talk about the poets and poetry of his native land, ancient and modern, is an experience which, when first encountered, gives the stranger quite a shock of agreeable surprise.
    W. SIKES
    Rambles and Studies in Old South Wales, 1881

Let's be kind to Anglo-Saxons,
To our neighbours let's be nice,
Welshmen, put aside all hatred,
Learn to love the bloody Sais!
    MEIC STEPHENS
    Our English Friends, 1963

The Welsh people are an animated, gesticulating people.
    WALT WHITMAN
    1889

I am not hot (unless the ice be hot:)
I am not cold (unless the fire be so:)
I am no Celt (or Celts say I am not:)
I am no Saxon, that at least I know!
   CONFESSIO JUVENIS
   Lament of a Trimmer

Sais Sais y gach yn ei bais,
Y Cymro glan y gach allan.
(The Saxon shites in his breech
The cleanly Briton in the hedge.)
   JAMES HOWELL
   British Proverbs Englished, 1659

Very gallant young fellows, these Celts, also born dialecticians ...
   KARL MARX
   Writing to Friedrich Engels in 1870

All Celtic people are, at heart, Communists.
   KEIR HARDIE, MP
   1907

The Celtic mind in its lonely moments is a tumbling sea of love, compassion, romanticism, and neurotic hates.
   RAY MILLAND
   Hollywood actor, born in South Wales

Taffy was a Welshman,
Taffy was a thief,
Taffy came to my house
And stole a leg of beef.

I went to Taffy's house,
Taffy was in bed,
I picked up a poker
And hit him on the head.
>   ANONYMOUS
>   18th century

Wherever I have been in Wales, I have experienced nothing but kindness and hospitality, and when I return to my own country I will say so.
>   GEORGE BORROW
>   *Wild Wales*, 1862

A Welshman has two sides to his nature. He has a strong urge to step on to the platform, to seek notice and applause, to hit the headlines. Some of us never conquer that: they go through life stepping on to platforms. Then there is the other quality, deeper, more real, more lasting – a childlike love of simple things, of the earth, of the mountains, of the home.
>   GERAINT GOODWIN (1903–41)

The Welsh Quotation Book

You Welsh! A race of mystical poets who have gone awry in some way.
>RHYS DAVIES
>*The Withered Root*, 1927

It is the occult secret of the most conservative, the most introverted, the most mysterious nation that has ever existed on the earth outside China.
>JOHN COWPER POWYS
>Writing about Wales in 1939

... they [the Welsh] don't straggle untidily like the English, who nowadays seem in such a mess ... There is no decadence in Wales ... There are rogues and ogres, true; there is scandalous behaviour. But the Celtic simplicity and wonder lies over all.
>RHYS DAVIES
>*Writing About the Welsh*, 1947

... the loquacious Welshman is a vivid gossiper, teller and creative weaver of tales ... In relating facts, a large allowance must be given to his imagination; a Welshman's horse is always descended from the beast ridden by Llewellyn the Great ...
>RHYS DAVIES
>*The Story of Wales*, 1943

The Welsh are the only people who are brave enough to tell a lie as if that lie were the truth.
CARADOC EVANS

The Welsh are a nation of toughs, rogues, and poetic humbugs, vivid in their speech, impulsive in behaviour, and riddled with a sly and belligerent tribalism.
V.S. PRITCHETT
New Statesman and Nation, 1939

The Welsh have remained to Englishmen a rather baffling breed, and bits of Wales and the Welsh are still an unravelled enigma, even to the Welsh themselves.
TREVOR FISHLOCK
Talking of Wales, 1976

Yes, there is a tension, an emotional tension, a tension between contrasting qualities and instincts. But yes, there is a Welshman hidden in many an Englishman, a Wales hidden in England. That is the enigma.
ENOCH POWELL, MP

We are warmhearted, ebullient, inquisitive, emotional, extrovert. Our blood is mixed. There is hardly a coloured face amongst us but Irish, Welsh, Spanish and English – also I believe Italian – have interbred. We are the people of the Welsh valleys. We shock the staid English.
HILDA EVANS
Western Mail

The Welsh Quotation Book

I have again and again been exceedingly amazed at the suspicion and distrust with which North Walians and South Walians, among the lower classes, regard each other.
J. HUGH EDWARDS
1907

Our compatriots in North Wales, where the Iberian strain is now thinnest, view us South Welshmen with a dubious eye ...
J.O. FRANCIS
1924

They're Arabs down there.
A North Walian commenting on South Wales

He was dark and lean, with a long South Welsh head narrowing downwards from a noble forehead to a sensitive mouth and strongly moulded jaw ... He had that slightly 'foreign' look which many handsome South Walians have, both in their own and other's estimation ...
Description of writer Alun Lewis (1915–44), 1941

In terms of sheer praying power, Wales must have a handsome credit balance in heaven!
TREVOR FISHLOCK
Wales and the Welsh, 1972

The Welsh Quotation Book

If we look at some aspects of Welshness we see that Wales remains a land of welcomes and ready hospitality, a country where the skills and pleasures of talking seem to count for more than in England's pub culture, and where children are encouraged to speak up and say their piece without precocity.
> TREVOR FISHLOCK
> *Talking of Wales*, 1976

Both sexes exceed any other nation in attention to their teeth, which they render like ivory, by constantly rubbing them with green hazel and wiping with a woollen cloth. For their better preservation, they abstain from hot meats, and eat only such as are cold, warm or temperate.

... the kitchen does not supply many dishes, nor highly seasoned incitements to eating.
> GIRALDUS CAMBRENSIS (GERALD OF WALES)
> *Description of Wales*, 12th century

The English soldiers, being accustomed to bread, could not do without it when they were in the land of the Welsh with nothing but meat or milk food on which that savage people is used to feed.
> THOMAS WYKES
> 1265

The Welsh Quotation Book

And once but taste o' the Welsh mutton,
Your English sheep's not worth a button:
  BEN JONSON
  For the Honour of Wales

As for the Diet of the Briton, it is not very delicate, neither is he curious in it; for if he should, his Appetite perhaps might cure his Nicety, and by pleasing his Palate, he may starve his Belly. A good Mess of Flummery, a Pair of Eggs he rejoices at as a Feast, especially if he may close his Stomach with toasted Cheese; a Morsel of which he hath great Kindness for. You may see him pictured sometimes ... with a Crescent of Cheese ... and his Hat adorned with a Plume of Leeks: Good edible Equipage! which, when Hunger pinches, he makes bold to nibble; he first eats his Cheese and his Leeks together, and for second Course, he devours his Horse.
  JOHN TORBUCK
  A Collection of Welsh Travels and Memoirs of Wales,
  1738

I devoted my attention to a brown loaf, but on cutting into it, was surprised to find a ball of carrotty coloured wool; and to what animal it had belonged, I was at a loss to determine.
HENRY WIGSTEAD
A Tour of North and South Wales in the Year 1797

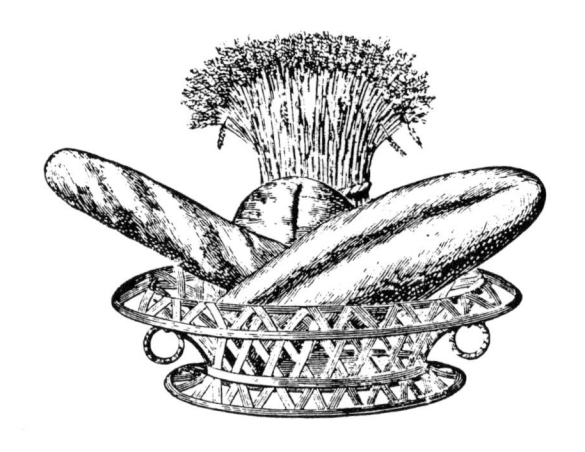

A Welshman and an Englishman disputed
   Which of their lands maintained the greatest state;
The Englishman the Welshman quite confuted
   Yet would the Welshman naught his brags abate.
'Ten cooks,' quoth he, 'In Wales one wedding sees,'
   'True,' quoth the other, 'each man toasts his cheese.'
   HENRY PARROT
   c. 1613

... the Welsh seem to have been particularly indifferent to the art of cooking. 'Tea and bread and butter' seems to be the national institution, and the amount of both which is consumed is amazing.
> COUNTESS MORPHY
> *English Recipes: Including the Traditional Dishes of Scotland, Ireland and Wales*, c. 1930

I find written among old jests how God made Saint Peter porter of heaven, and that God of His goodness, soon after His Passion, suffered many men to come to the kingdom of heaven with small deserving; at which time there was in heaven a great company of Welshmen which with their cracking and babbling troubled all the others. Wherefore God said to Saint Peter that He was weary of them and that He fain would have them out of heaven. To whom Saint Peter said, 'Good Lord, I warrant you, that shall be done.'

Wherefore Saint Peter went out of heaven-gates and cried with a loud voice, '*Caws pob*' – that is as much as to say 'roasted cheese' – which thing the Welshmen hearing, ran out of heaven a great pace. And when Saint Peter saw them all out, he suddenly went into heaven and locked the door, and so sparred all the Welshmen out.
> Merry Tales, Wittie Questions and Quicke Answeres, 1567

The Welsh Quotation Book

WELCH RABBIT (i.e. a Welch rare bit). Bread and cheese toasted. See RABBIT. – The Welch are said to be so remarkably fond of cheese, that in cases of difficulty their midwives apply a piece of toasted cheese to the *janua vitae*, to attract and entice the young Taffy, who on smelling it makes most vigorous efforts to come forth.
   FRANCIS GROSE
   A Classical Dictionary of the Vulgar Tongue, 1785

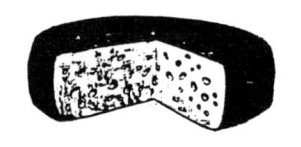

The way to make a Welch-man thirst for blisse
And say his prayers dayly on his knees:
Is to perswade him, that most certaine 'tis,
The Moone is made of nothing but greene Cheese.
And hee'l desire of God no greater boone,
But place in heaven to feed upon the Moone.
   JOHN TAYLOR
   Epigram, in *The Sculler*, 1612

The Welshwoman who has mastered the mysteries of the broth, and is acquainted with the various ways in which oatmeal may be made palatable and digestible, may be said to have, for her purposes, finished her education in cookery.
> D.J. NICHOLAS
> 1907

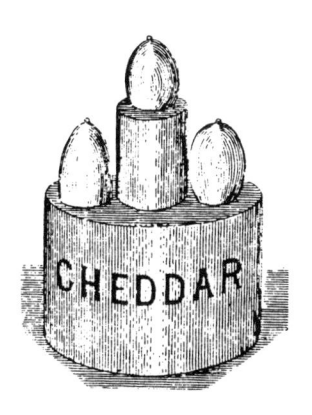

The Welsh have always been partial to cheese and forecasts of doom. In my native valley we had a patriarchal neighbour who, through mouthfuls of roasted Cheddar, gave us regular news of the world's impending end.
> GWYN THOMAS
> *Western Mail*

The Welsh Quotation Book

Never Forget Your Welsh.
    Slogan advertising Welsh bitter beer

Rugby is ... the game of the Welshman
    The Welsh Outlook
    1914

As every Welsh rugby fan knows, no match is more important than the one against England. Regardless of whether ... the match is at the Arms Park or Twickenham, the confrontation between the Old Enemy is always special, something to savour, and greeted with eager anticipation by player and supporter alike.
    GARETH EDWARDS
    Most Memorable Matches, 1984

The hankering for kicking 'the black ball' has fallen like a plague on the boys of the south. Day and night, for the poor and the wealthy, the religious and the irreligious, football is the talking point ... And several of the daily and weekly newspapers employ correspondents to cover it, and set aside long columns for the purpose of giving detailed reports of such bestial sports.
>	A comment on rugby published in the Welsh
>	Language newspaper, *Y Faner*, in 1885

Rugby, as played by the Welsh, is not a game. It is a tribal mystery.
>	GWYN THOMAS
>	1965

Make me content
With some sweetness
From Wales
Whose nightingales
Have no wings.
    EDWARD THOMAS (1878–1917)
    Words

No alien hearts may know that magic, which acquaints
Thy soul with splendid passion, a great fire of dreams;
Thine heart with lovelier sorrow, than the wistful sea.
Voices of Celtic singers and of Celtic Saints
Live on the ancient air: their royal sunlight gleams
On moorland Merioneth and on sacred Dee.
    LIONEL JOHNSON
    Wales, 1890

Merionethshire, the land of all that is beautiful in nature, and all that is lovely in woman.
    THOMAS LOVE PEACOCK
    Crotchet Castle, 1831

In respect of Milford Haven all the Havens under the Heavens are inconsiderable.
    JOHN TAYLOR
    A Short Relation of a Long Journey, 1653

The Welsh Quotation Book

The inhabitants, [of Merionethshire] who for the most part wholy betake themselves to breeding & feeding of cattaile, and live upon white meates, as butter, cheese &c. ... are for stature, cleere complexion, goodly feature, & lineaments of body inferiour to no nation in Britain: but they have an ill name among their neighbours, for being to forward in the wanton love of women, and that proceeding from their idlenesse.
    WILLIAM CAMDEN
    Britain, 1610 (Philemon Holland's translation)

Evening on the olden, the golden sea of Wales
When the first star shivers
and the last waves pale:
Oh evening dreams.
    JAMES ELROY FLECKER (1884–1915)
    The Gates of Damascus

'Tis said, O Cambria, thou hast tried in vain
To form great poets, and the cause is plain.
Ap-Jones, Ap-Jenkins, and Ap-Evans sound
Among thy sons, but no Apollos found.
    ANONYMOUS
    Epigrams Ancient and Modern, ed. Revd John Booth, 1863

The Welsh Quotation Book

I continued along the great road; and, within two miles of *Mold*, hung long over the charming vale which opens with exquisite beauty from *Fron*, ... *Cambria* here lays aside her majestic air, and condescends to assume a gentler form ...
    THOMAS PENNANT
    Tours in Wales, 1773–6

May the inhabitants be like the land they live in; which appears worse than it is, seemingly barren and really fruitful.
    THOMAS FULLER
    History of the Worthies of England, 1662
    Of Anglesey

A part of this county is peopled by Flemings, placed there by King Henry the First, who was no less politic than charitable therein; for such Flemings, being driven out of their own country by an irruption of the ocean, were fixed here to defend the land given them against the Welch; and their country is called Little England beyond Wales. This mindeth me of a passage betwixt a Welch and English-man, the former boasting Wales in all respects beyond England; to whom the other returned, 'He had heard of an England beyond Wales, but never of a Wales beyond England.'
    THOMAS FULLER
    History of the Worthies of England, 1662
    Of Pembrokeshire

The Welsh Quotation Book

'The cheapest country in England!' How much people are deceived at a distance! – its cheapness is all a flim-flam, and nothing remains as it used to be, but its glorious scenery.
>THOMAS MOORE
>Letter to Miss Dalby, 1812

The Devil lives in the middle of Wales.
>DANIEL DEFOE
>*A Tour Through the Whole Island of Britain*, 1724

Now I perceive the devil understands Welsh.
>WILLIAM SHAKESPEARE
>*Henry IV, Part 1*

They value themselves much upon their antiquity: The antient race of their houses, and families, and the like; and above all, upon their antient heroes: their King Caractacus Owen ap Tudor, Prince Lewellin, and the like noblemen and princes of British extraction; and as they believe their country to be the pleasantest and most agreeable in the world, so you cannot oblige them more, than to make them think you believe so too.
>DANIEL DEFOE
>*A Tour Through the Whole Island of Britain*, 1724

A patriot, and so true, that it to death him greeves
To heare his Wales disgrac't: and on the Saxons swords
Oft hazardeth his life, ere with reprochful words
His language or his leeke hee'le stand to heare abus'd
   MICHAEL DRAYTON
   Poly-Olbion, 1612

Our Caernarvonshire Hills looked very respectable after seeing both Alps & Appenines; we agreed that Penmanmawr was about the size of Vesuvius, & looked not unlike it one Evening from Bangor Ferry.
   HESTER LYNCH THRALE/PIOZZI
   Thraliana

All subtle feelings are discerned by Welsh eyes when untroubled by any mental agitation ... I may observe that there is human nature and Welsh nature.
   GEORGE MEREDITH
   Sandra Belloni, 1864

Here is a theme that never fails,
   To write or talk upon.
The Undersigned has been in Wales,
   Jonah was but in One –
   THOMAS HOOD
   Quoted in Henry Crabb Robinson, *Diary*, 26 July 1836

Abergeley is a large Village on the Sea Coast – Walking on the sea sands – I was surprized to see a number of fine Women bathing promiscuously with men and boys – *perfectly* naked! Doubtless the citadels of their Chastity are so impregnably strong, that they need not the ornamental Outworks of Modesty.
    S.T. COLERIDGE
    Letter to Henry Martin, 22 July 1794

  Lo here I sit at holy head,
  With muddy ale and mouldy bread:
  I'm fastened both by wind and tide,
  I see the ships at anchor ride.
  All Christian vittals stink of fish,
  I'm where my enemyes would wish …
    JONATHAN SWIFT
    Holyhead, 25 September 1727

Llangathen (Dyfed)
  'Tis now the raven's bleak abode;
  'Tis now th'apartment of the toad;
  And there the fox securely feeds;
  And there the poisonous adder breeds,
  Conceal'd in ruins, moss and weeds;
  While ever and anon there falls
  Huge heaps of hoary, moulder'd walls …
    JOHN DYER
    Grongar Hill, 1727

The Welsh Quotation Book

At Denbigh is a ruined Castle – it surpasses every thing I could have conceived – I wandered there an hour and a half last evening. Two well drest young men were walking there – Come – says one – I'll play my flute – 'twill be romantic! Bless thee for the thought, Man of Genius & Sensibility! I exclaimed – and pre-attuned my heartstring to tremulous emotion. He sat adown (the moon just peering) amid the most awful part of the Ruins – and – romantic Youth! struck up the affecting Tune of *Mrs Casey*!
    S.T. COLERIDGE
    Letter to Robert Southey, 13 July 1794

I shall be loth to leave Denbigh – 'tis such an admirable *Thinking-Place*.
    HESTER LYNCH THRALE/PIOZZI
    Thraliana

The older the welshman the more madman.
    JAMES HOWELL
    British Proverbs Englished, in *Lexicon Tetraglotton ... with another Volume of the Choicest Proverbs*, 1659

In Wales – they make calling one another Liar's &c – necessary vent-holes to the sulphureous Fumes of the Temper!
    S.T. COLERIDGE
    Letter to Robert Southey, 13 July 1794

The Welsh Quotation Book

Now good Mister Spictatur of *Crete Prittain*, you must know it, there iss in Caernarvonshire a fery Pig Mountain, the Clory of all Wales, which iss named *Penmainmaure*, and you must also know, it iss no great Journey on Foot from me; but the Road is stony and bad for Shoes.
    JOSEPH ADDISON
    Spectator, no.227, 20 November 1711

Wales is a bit crazed on the subject of religion.
    GEORGE BORROW
    Wild Wales, 1862

If it should ever be your misfortune to have spent Sunday in Wales, always get to windward when the chapels are disgorging the faithful.
    ARTHUR TYSSILIO JOHNSON
    The Perfidious Welshman, 1910

If we are to understand the history of Wales, and to know the Welshman's soul, we have to start with the mountains.

It is not race or language that has made Wales a separate country and the Welsh a peculiar people. Wales owes its separate existence to its mountains; it is to the mountains that the Welsh people owe their national characteristics.
    OWEN M. EDWARDS
    Observations made in the 1890s

The difference between England and Wales is that England consists of an upper class, a middle class and a democracy, while Wales is a democracy pure and simple.
>T.W.H. CROSLAND
>*Taffy was a Welshman*, 1912

Probably the oldest wisdom in Wales was that wisest and most ancient of all human wisdom; namely that it is within the power of the will and the imagination to destroy and recreate the world.
>JOHN COWPER POWYS
>*Autobiography*, 1934

British culture is a fact, but the English contribution to it is very small ... There is actually no such thing as 'English' culture; a few individuals may be highly cultured, but the people as a whole are crass.
>From a document inviting subscriptions to *Wales* (a literary pamphlet), 1937

I call this habit the leekiness of the Welsh literary Kitchen garden. That garden is small, and if we will go on rearing the Welsh national vegetable all over it, there just won't be room to grow potatoes to live on, saying nothing of the rarer asparagus or sea kale. To put it plainly, I would like to read a Welsh author ... not mentioning (a) the harmonium (b) Eisteddfods.
>MARGIAD EVANS
>On literary criticism, 1937

The Welsh Quotation Book

They began singing. Instead of the usual music-hall songs they sang Welsh hymns, each man taking a part. The Welsh always sang when pretending not to be scared: it kept them steady. And they never sang out of tune.
>ROBERT GRAVES
>*Goodbye to All That*, 1929

Blessed is a world that sings,
Gentle are its songs.
>T. GWYNN JONES
>In the programme for the 1947 Llangollen International Musical Eisteddfod, held to help heal the wounds of war

When I see the enthusiasm these Eisteddfods can awaken in your whole people, and then think of the tastes, the literature, the amusements of our own lower and middle classes, I am filled with admiration.
> MATTHEW ARNOLD
> 1866

If people want to sing, dance, become crowned bards and dress up in night-shirts, why not? It's just that it means so much to some people and so little to others. In my particular neck of the woods, it falls far short of 'Come Dancing' and the International Horse Show in terms of appeal.
> HERBERT WILLIAMS
> *South Wales Echo*

... the National Eisteddfod ... is racial intolerance set to music.
> IAN SKIDMORE
> 1986

It is showy, it is a little sentimental, some people find it, with its invented antiquities of ritual and costume, rather silly; but it is unmistakably alive.
> JAN MORRIS
> Commenting on the 1982 National Eisteddfod

The Welsh Quotation Book

The bardic sword was three times unsheathed. Barefoot maidenettes skipped behind the horn of plenty. ('Isadora, where are you now that we need you?' moaned a lady from San Francisco, and adjusted her green stetson and tartan apron.) ... That bardic ceremony, like the whole week's events at the National Eisteddfod, was 100% sincere and 100% synthetic. As the Plaid Cymru lads (Benetton sweatshirts, miners' union badges) will remind you, the proceedings do not go back, bard to bard, to Arthurian antiquity but are about contemporaneous with the building of Brighton Pavilion for the Prince Regent.
    SUNDAY TIMES
    Report on the 1984 National Eisteddfod

D.W. Griffith seemed almost inhuman: he was of Welsh extraction, and the Welsh are a very peculiar breed – poetic, unpredictable, remote, and fiercely independent.
    ANITA LOOS
    Writing about the pioneer film director D.W. Griffith

> There was a young man of Porthcawl
> Who thought he was Samson or Saul:
> These thoughts so obscure
> Were due to the brewer,
> And not to his ego at all.
>   A.G. PRYS-JONES
>   *A Little Nonsense*, 1954

I was educated not at Oxford but in the back seats of the Plaza in Swansea.
WYNFORD VAUGHAN-THOMAS (1908–87)

There was an old lady of Wales
who lived upon oysters and snails
Upon growing a shell,
She exclaimed, 'It is well,
Now I'll never wear bonnets or veils.'
ANONYMOUS

The Royal Variety Command Performance which made last Sunday the longest Sabbath since the Lord's first Day of Rest, must be republicanism's most powerful secret weapon.
GWYN THOMAS
Western Mail

We started drinking at seven
And went out for a breather at ten,
And all the stars in heaven
Said, Go back and drink again.
HARRI WEBB
Big Night, 1963

That Investiture, amid the cheers of the Welsh and the grovelling of archbishops and bishops and the leaders of all the Welsh denominations, was the darkest hour of the sixties.
>SAUNDERS LEWIS
>Writing about the Investiture of Prince Charles as Prince of Wales in 1969

Among our ancient mountains,
And from our lovely vales,
Oh, let the prayer re-echo
'God bless the Prince of Wales!'
>GEORGE LINLEY (1798–1865)
>*God Bless the Prince of Wales*

I've played the lot, a homosexual, a sadistic gangster, princes, a saint, the lot. All that's left is a Carry On film. My last ambition.
>RICHARD BURTON
>1972

Outside the family, being Welsh was the greatest blessing he had and he held to it.
>MELVYN BRAGG
>*Rich*
>On Richard Burton

The Welsh Quotation Book

I know that practically the only growth industry in Wales has been the invention of its own history; forged – in every sense of the word – in the fires of its own powerful fancy.
    IAN SKIDMORE
    1986

Welsh women are certainly saner than their counterparts in England and America.
    PETER STEAD
    BBC Wales, 1993

We shall live out this century in a rising tide of drink, religion and violence.
    GWYN THOMAS
    1968

FINIS.